THURGOOD MARSHALL

BY JOAN STOLTMAN

Gareth Stevens
PUBLISHING

Please visit our website, www.garethstevens.com. For a free color catalog of all our high-quality books, call toll free 1-800-542-2595 or fax 1-877-542-2596.

Library of Congress Cataloging-in-Publication Data

Names: Stoltman, Joan, author.
Title: Thurgood Marshall / Joan Stoltman.
Description: New York : Gareth Stevens Publishing, 2019. | Series: Heroes of
    black history | Includes index.
Identifiers: LCCN 2018022959| ISBN 9781538230213 (library bound) | ISBN
    9781538231333 (pbk.) | ISBN 9781538233139 (6 pack)
Subjects: LCSH: Marshall, Thurgood, 1908-1993–Juvenile literature. | United
    States. Supreme Court–Biography–Juvenile literature. | African American
    lawyers–Biography–Juvenile literature. | African American
    judges–Biography–Juvenile literature.
Classification: LCC KF8745.M34 S76 2019 | DDC 347.73/2634 [B] –dc23
LC record available at https://lccn.loc.gov/2018022959

First Edition

Published in 2019 by
Gareth Stevens Publishing
111 East 14th Street, Suite 349
New York, NY 10003

Copyright © 2019 Gareth Stevens Publishing

Designer: Katelyn E. Reynolds
Editor: Joshua Turner

Photo credits: Cover, pp. 1 (Thurgood Marshall), 11, 21, 25 Bettmann/Getty Images; cover, pp. 1–32 (background image) Brandon Bourdages/Shutterstock.com; p. 5 (top) PhotoQuest/Getty Images; pp. 7, 9 Library of Congress/Corbis/VCG via Getty Images; p. 13 Cornell Capa/The LIFE Picture Collection/Getty Images; p. 17 Carl Iwasaki/The LIFE Images Collection/Getty Images; p. 19 Hank Walker/The LIFE Picture Collection/Getty Images; pp. 5 (both bottom), 15, 23, 27 courtesy of the Library of Congress; p. 29 Terry Ashe/The LIFE Images Collection/Getty Images.

Printed in the United States of America

CPSIA compliance information: Batch #CW19GS: For further information contact Gareth Stevens, New York, New York at 1-800-542-2595.

CONTENTS

Words in the glossary appear in **bold** type the first time they are used in the text.

ARGUING ALL HIS LIFE

Thurgood Marshall was born in 1908 in Baltimore, Maryland. He was named after his great-grandfather, who had escaped slavery and fought for the North during the Civil War. His mother was a teacher and passed on to Marshall how important education was. His father worked several jobs and taught Marshall about hard work and pride.

His father often brought Marshall and his brother, Aubrey, to court to listen to cases. Then they'd return home and **debate** cases, laws, politics, and current events at the dinner table. Marshall loved arguing and debating, and often he got in trouble for it at school. Even still, he graduated from high school early.

SEGREGATION

Maryland had been a slave state before the Civil War. After the war, **segregation** laws were passed in Maryland and the South to keep blacks and whites separate in schools, staircases, trains, hospitals, bathrooms, and more. The places for whites were always much nicer than those for blacks, even though they were supposed to be equal.

For young black people like Thurgood (top) who grew up in the early 1900s, segregation was the only way of life they knew.

AN EDUCATION

Thurgood and his brother worked for a kind white man during high school. The man saw a great deal of promise in them and even agreed to pay for their college education! But, he died before this happened. Determined to still go to college, Thurgood, as well as his family, sacrificed a great deal to make that happen.

Thurgood and his brother both went to Lincoln University in Pennsylvania, the oldest black college in the country. Thurgood worked several jobs to be able to afford to attend this famous school, and his mother even sold her wedding rings to help him keep up with payments.

IMPORTANT AMENDMENTS

After the Civil War, two **amendments** were made to the **Constitution** to provide blacks with equal rights. The Fourteenth Amendment defines citizenship as being born in the country and promises equal protection under the law for all citizens. The Fifteenth Amendment gave black men the right to vote. Both were ignored by Southern states soon after they were passed.

Thurgood went to school with many famous people, including poet Langston Hughes and the future president of Ghana!

7

LAW SCHOOL

Thurgood knew his love of and skill for debate would make him a great **lawyer**. Since he wasn't allowed to attend the nearby law school because he was black, he traveled an hour each way every day to Washington, DC, to attend Howard University.

Thurgood flourished under the **mentoring** of the school's dean, Charles Houston. He often brought Thurgood to meetings of the NAACP (National Association for the Advancement of Colored People). Soon, Thurgood was assisting Houston on NAACP cases. When Thurgood graduated first in his law school class, he was given the chance to study constitutional law at Harvard University. He turned it down because he wanted to get in the courtroom and start fighting.

THE NAACP

In 1909, black leader W. E. B. DuBois and several others founded the NAACP to fight against police violence, the jailing of **innocent** people, and other problems black people were having in the South. By the 1940s, NAACP lawyers worked on large cases that changed society, such as voting, employment, and housing rights.

Thurgood couldn't attend the University of Maryland Law School in Baltimore, Maryland, because he was black. Five years later, one of the first cases he won forced the university to admit black students.

THE FIGHT BEGINS

In 1933, Thurgood opened a law office in Baltimore, often helping the NAACP's Baltimore chapter. In 1935, Charles Houston became the NAACP's first lead lawyer at its main office in New York City. Houston's plan to end segregation was to organize a series of court cases that would prove segregation wasn't constitutional.

In 1936, Thurgood moved to New York to assist these efforts. Within a few years, Thurgood took over for Houston by heading up a new, separate organization called the NAACP **Legal** Defense and Educational Fund. Thurgood continued to organize the NAACP's court actions against segregation until 1961!

WHO WAS CHARLES HOUSTON?

Houston was one of the lead lawyers in the early years of the civil rights movement. He believed the Constitution needed to be **interpreted** for modern times, not the times in which it was written. He used the law and the Constitution as tools for change, working for the NAACP for nearly 15 years.

Thurgood's cases were strengthened by his full understanding of the effects of segregation. He came to that understanding by, among other things, studying **race riots**, including the 1943 riot in Detroit, Michigan, shown above.

ONE BY ONE

Thurgood and Houston's plan was to end segregation by attacking each type of segregation one by one. Each case started with a Southern jury or judge who would decide to maintain segregation. Then Thurgood would petition, or ask, the Supreme Court to review that local court's decision. The Supreme Court makes decisions, called rulings, by interpreting the Constitution, and its rulings apply to the whole country.

Thurgood brought 32 cases to the Supreme Court with the NAACP, more than anyone else in history! These cases included those about black rights to property, housing, travel, trial, jury, and voting. He was able to show time and again that black people weren't treated equally, proving that segregation **violated** the Fourteenth Amendment.

PLESSY V. FERGUSON

Segregation was legally protected by an 1896 Supreme Court ruling. In the case of *Plessy v. Ferguson*, Homer Plessy wanted Louisiana to end segregation on trains. The Supreme Court, however, agreed with Louisiana, deciding that public facilities provided for blacks could be "separate but equal" to those provided to whites.

Thurgood worked to get the Supreme Court to overturn, or rule against, *Plessy v. Ferguson* for much of his career as a lawyer.

MR. CIVIL RIGHTS

Thousands of black people from all over the country needed legal help. At times, the NAACP legal team worked nearly 450 cases at once, with Thurgood overseeing. But of all those cases, Thurgood could lead only a handful himself. He had to choose cases that would fit into his planned attack of legal segregation in the Supreme Court.

For his cases, Thurgood often organized planning meetings. He'd invite 20 to 30 trusted lawyers and NAACP workers to review the case. After days of debate, Thurgood would have several solid ideas about how the case could be argued.

A CASE LOST, A LESSON LEARNED

In 1940, the Supreme Court ruled that when a person confesses to a crime after being beaten by police, the confession isn't legal. In 1941, a black man named W. D. Lyons had been beaten until he confessed, and yet the Supreme Court ruled that Lyons had to go to prison. Thurgood had defended Lyons, and the case reminded him that there was still work ahead.

To fight in court against **racist** judges and police in the South was very dangerous. Thurgood was often warned that his work could get him killed.

THE BIG CASE

The most famous case Thurgood argued was 1954's *Brown v. Board of Education of Topeka*, which ended legal segregation in schools. Thurgood thought that attacking education segregation was the strongest way to prove that any segregation violated the Fourteenth Amendment. Thurgood's other wins in the Supreme Court provided a strong legal **foundation** against education segregation.

Thurgood spent 4 years on the legal argument for this case. He ended his arguments by reminding the Supreme Court justices of all the segregation laws they'd already done away with. Every single justice voted in agreement to end education segregation. Separate was no longer thought to be equal!

SLOW CHANGE

Brown v. Board of Education's ruling said that school segregation needed to be undone "with all deliberate speed." Thurgood thought it would take 5 years. But the 21 states with education segregation were slow to change their practices because they weren't given a firm date by which to end them. Some places ignored the ruling altogether. School segregation is still considered a problem today.

Brown v. Board of Education included the cases of several black children, shown above. Thurgood said: "Unless our children begin to learn together, there is little hope that our people will ever begin to live together."

NAACP V. ALABAMA

Brown v. Board of Education was a case about education segregation, but the Supreme Court's ruling said that all segregation was illegal. Soon after, several Southern states tried to push the NAACP out of the South. One method was to pass out names of NAACP members to the public, which often got members beaten up and even fired from jobs.

Alabama chose a different method, and tried to ban the NAACP in 1958. Thurgood took the case to the Supreme Court, and every single justice agreed that this violated the First Amendment. They also voted down making NAACP members' names public.

THE MOVEMENT GROWS

Many people felt that if the South could disobey the Supreme Court's *Brown v. Board of Education* ruling, then they too could disobey laws they felt were unfair. However, Thurgood didn't like this method of trying to make changes because he didn't believe in breaking the law to prove a point!

Supreme Court
building

Law students continue to study
Thurgood's legal arguments today.

JOINING THE FEDERAL GOVERNMENT

By 1961, Thurgood was ready to help the country in a new way. President John F. Kennedy chose him to become a judge for the Second Circuit of the US Court of Appeals. But first, the Senate had to approve him for the position in a vote. Southern senators stopped Thurgood from officially getting the position for nearly a year. When Thurgood finally won the Senate's vote, he became the second black person ever to serve as a circuit court judge.

In the Second Circuit, Thurgood made over 112 rulings. None of his rulings have ever been reversed, or overturned, by the Supreme Court!

WHAT ARE CIRCUIT COURTS?

Circuit courts are part of the federal court system. They decide whether or not the law was interpreted correctly in trials decided by lower courts. Each case that makes it to a circuit court is reviewed by three judges, not a jury. The United States is broken up into 12 circuits, with the Second Circuit covering New York, Vermont, and Connecticut.

Thurgood Jr.

Thurgood's wife, Cecilia

John W.

Thurgood's sons would also serve the federal government in Washington, DC. Thurgood Marshall Jr. was a lawyer and worked in the White House under President Bill Clinton. John W. Marshall served as the US Marshals Service director after being Virginia's Secretary of Public Safety.

21

Four years later, President Lyndon B. Johnson made Thurgood the first black solicitor general. Several of the cases he fought in the Supreme Court during this time were civil rights cases. Thurgood won 14 of the 19 cases he fought in his position as solicitor general.

In 1967, President Johnson looked to Thurgood to lead the country's federal court system once again. This time, he was appointed, or chosen, as the first black man to sit on the Supreme Court. After 5 days of questioning, 69 of 80 Senators voted for him to take on this new position as one of the nine Supreme Court justices.

THE SOLICITOR GENERAL

The solicitor general is the lawyer who represents the federal government's side in front of the Supreme Court. As the third highest officer in the Justice Department, the only people higher than the solicitor general are the president and the attorney general. Whoever holds this job is sometimes called the "tenth justice."

Thurgood's successes as a lawyer often came because of just how tirelessly he worked to prepare for cases. Many lawyers who fought against him never even had a chance!

23

THE FIRST BLACK JUSTICE

During his early years as a Supreme Court justice, Thurgood saw many cases about segregation and racism. His years of experience as a lawyer gave him a special view of the law. He knew how the law made a difference in people's lives. Thurgood worked hard to always remind his fellow justices to think about what the Supreme Court's rulings would do for real people.

Throughout his career as a justice, Thurgood **consistently** pushed for individual rights like free speech, education, voting, privacy, and fair police and court treatment. Through his votes, Thurgood always supported affirmative action for blacks and other racial groups, women, and poor people.

AFFIRMATIVE ACTION

Supporters of affirmative action believe that the lack of opportunities in past generations still give certain people more success and other people less success today. Affirmative action supporters want hiring and college-acceptance decisions to give advantages to groups of people who didn't have them before. People still debate using affirmative action today.

While a justice, Thurgood created a system for interpreting the Fourteenth Amendment. It figured out what the current needs for the government were and weighed them against the current needs of the people. The Supreme Court didn't officially use Thurgood's system, but the ideas behind it helped decide several major civil rights cases in the 1970s!

25

THE GREAT DISSENTER

Early on, Thurgood's votes were often part of the majority. But soon enough he'd become known as the "Great Dissenter" as presidents appointed new justices whose views he didn't share. Because Thurgood believed in the power of his vote and his voice, he often wrote strongly worded dissents against the Supreme Court majority's rulings.

WHAT IS A DISSENT?

The majority-voting justices have their views expressed in a document called the opinion. The opinion is the official ruling of the Supreme Court. Justices not in the majority express their views in a document called a dissent. Dissents can and do change justices' votes, and sometimes enough votes are changed that the dissent becomes the majority!

Thurgood dissented strongly whenever the Supreme Court's opinions limited individual rights, affirmative action, free speech, and the rights of criminals. Perhaps his biggest fight was against the **death penalty**. He believed it violated the Eighth Amendment, which protects criminals from cruel and unusual punishment. He even wrote more than 150 dissents in death penalty cases the Supreme Court chose not to hear.

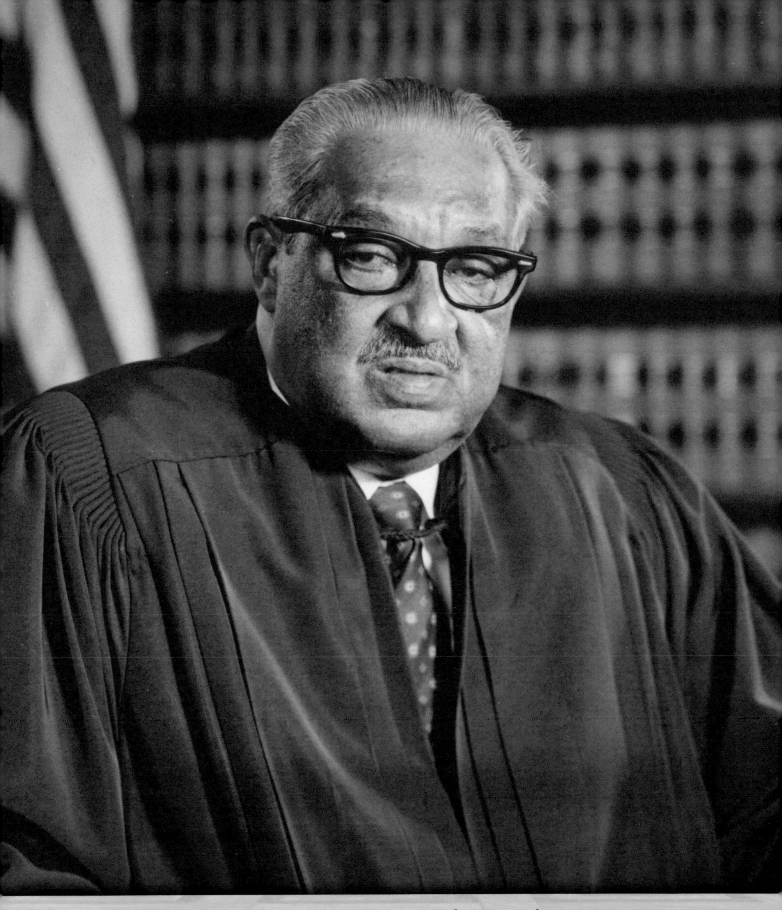

Thurgood wrote 322 opinions, 363 dissents, and 84 concurrences. A concurrence is an official record of points that didn't make it into the opinion but that support its outcome. Dissents and concurrences make it possible for all voices to become part of the Supreme Court's official records.

27

NEVER QUIT

Failing health forced Thurgood to retire after over 20 years as a justice and nearly 60 years of work. When Thurgood died soon after his retirement, he was honored as much more than a Supreme Court justice.

Thurgood's efforts supported human rights, not just black rights. He was committed to showing that the Constitution could work for the people as long as its interpretation changed with the country. Through the court system, Thurgood moved forward the world's understanding of the law, showing that it must change whenever it no longer serves the people.

Thurgood Marshall leaves a legacy of hard work, determination, and success that should inspire all people for years to come.

THE NAACP TODAY

NAACP lawyers are still hard at work today in the fight against racism. They've recently organized cases against laws limiting voting rights, hotels acting against black college students, hiring that ignores affirmative action, and illegal housing policies. They also work to fight modern education segregation in the form of poorly funded public schools in inner cities.

Thurgood always kept a copy of
the Constitution in his pocket. 29

GLOSSARY

amendment: a change or addition to a constitution

consistently: having to do with always acting or behaving the same way

constitution: the basic laws by which a country or state is governed

death penalty: death as a punishment given by a court of law for a very serious crime

debate: an argument or public discussion. Also, to argue a side.

foundation: something, such as an idea, a principle, or a fact, that provides support for something

innocent: not guilty of a crime or other wrong act

interpret: to explain the meaning of something as you see it

lawyer: someone whose job it is to help people with their questions and problems with the law

legal: of or relating to the law

mentor: to provide advice and support to a less experienced person

race riot: a violent fight between people of different races, caused by racial anger or hatred

racist: poor treatment of or violence against people because of their race. Also, the belief that some races of people are better than others.

segregation: the forced separation of races or classes

violate: to do something that is not allowed by a law

FOR MORE INFORMATION

BOOKS

Mortensen, Lori. *Voices of the Civil Rights Movement.* North Mankato, MN: Capstone, 2015.

Pinkney, Andrea Davis, and Brian Pinkney. *Hand in Hand: Ten Black Men Who Changed America.* New York: Jump at the Sun Books, 2012.

WEBSITES

Biographies of the Robes
www.thirteen.org/wnet/supremecourt/pop_biographies/index.html
Read about other Supreme Court justices who have served during the history of the United States.

History and Biography
thurgoodmarshall.com/thurgood-marshall-videos/
Check out videos about Thurgood Marshall throughout his life.

History of the Supreme Court
supremecourthistory.org/history_courthistory.html
Read all about the Supreme Court.

INDEX